PETE ROSE

PETE ROSE
Baseball's Charlie Hustle

Nathan Aaseng

 Lerner Publications Company ■ Minneapolis

ACKNOWLEDGEMENTS: The photographs are reproduced through the courtesy of: pp. 1, 7, 38, 39, 44, Leo S. Matkins, News Journal Company; p. 2, Cincinnati Reds; pp. 6, 20, 21, 30, L. D. Fullerton; pp. 8, 33, Richard Pilling; pp. 14, 23, 25, 27, 28, 42, Wide World Photos, Inc.; pp. 17, 19, Carl Skalak, Jr.; p. 31, Jim Denney; pp. 37, 41, Paul H. Roedig, Philadelphia Phillies; pp. 45 (top), 48 (bottom left), Detroit Tigers; p. 45 (bottom left), Atlanta Braves; pp. 45 (bottom right), 48 (top right), St. Louis Cardinals; p. 45 (top left), Philadelphia Phillies; pp. 46 (top right), 47 (top right), Cleveland Indians; pp. 46 (bottom left), 47 (bottom left), Pittsburgh Pirates; p. 46 (bottom right), National Baseball Hall of Fame and Museum, Inc.; p. 47 (top left), New York Giants; p. 47 (bottom right), Boston Red Sox; p. 48 (top left), George Brace. Front cover photo: Bill Smith Photography. Back cover photo: Cincinnati Reds.

To Grandma

LIBRARY OF CONGRESS CATALOGING IN PUBLICATION DATA

Aaseng, Nathan.
  Pete Rose, baseball's Charlie Hustle.

  (The Achievers)
  Includes index.
  SUMMARY: A biography of the major league baseball player who is one of the select group to have hit 3,000 times and have had 10 seasons of more than 200 hits.

  1. Rose, Pete, 1941-   —Juvenile literature. 2. Baseball players—United States—Biography—Juvenile literature. [1. Rose, Pete, 1941- 2. Baseball players] I. Title. II. Series: Achievers.

GV865.R65A63   796.357'092'4 [B] [92]   79-27377
ISBN 0-8225-0480-4 lib. bdg.

Manufactured in the United States of America.

International Standard Book Number: 0-8225-0480-4
Library of Congress Catalog Card Number: 79-27377

1   2   3   4   5   6   7   8   9   10   86   85   84   83   82   81

PETE ROSE

When Peter Edward Rose finally retires from baseball, so might his uniform. Baseball's best players often have one of their uniforms "retired" to a special place for visitors to see. But unless Pete's shirt and pants are smeared with dirt, they will not look like the real thing. Fans are used to seeing his famous headfirst belly flops as he slides into a base. The dirty uniform is a trademark of the way Pete Rose plays baseball.

Nicknamed Charlie Hustle by his fellow players, Pete has worked and scrambled to be as good as he is. And he has enjoyed every minute of it. When he prances onto the baseball diamond, he looks as excited as a boy coming home after the last day of school for the year.

As captain of the Cincinnati Reds, Pete takes his team's lineup card to the umpire's pre-game meeting at home plate.

Pete takes a rip against the St. Louis Cardinals. During this game in 1979, Pete stroked hit #200. This gave him 10 seasons of 200 or more hits to break Ty Cobb's record.

Pete is also one of baseball's top hitters. No batter in the game's history has piled up more 200-hit seasons than Rose. Three times he has had the highest batting average in the National League! Some say he has done more with his ability than any other baseball player.

7

Standing deep in the batter's box, Pete gets ready to swing.

Pete learned to give his best in sports in the small town of Anderson Ferry, Ohio, where he was born in 1941. He could have had no better example than his own father, Harry "Pete" Rose. Harry Rose was an all-around athlete who was not afraid to knock heads in semi-pro football and baseball. Some people say that after Harry broke his hip during a football play, he still tried to crawl downfield to make the tackle. No matter how tired he was after a game, Harry would make a point of charging full speed up the hill to his home.

Mr. Rose made sure his son Pete kept close to sports. One day Mr. Rose went out to buy Pete's sister a pair of shoes. He came home with a pair of boxing gloves for three-year-old Pete instead! Mrs. Rose wondered if there weren't something a toddler could use more than boxing gloves!

With his father's help, Pete was soon good at most sports, including football and boxing. But because of his small size, he worked hardest at baseball. Mr. Rose watched Pete closely and taught him how to *switch-hit*. In other words, if the pitcher was right-handed, Pete would bat left-handed. Faced with a left-handed pitcher, he turned around and batted right-handed. Switch-hitting is useful for pro ball-players. Curve balls from a right-handed pitcher head straight toward a right-handed batter before curving out and over the plate. Many batters have a hard time trying to hit a ball that seems to be aimed right at them. A switch-hitter never faces this problem. Even though Pete could bat from both sides, he felt much more comfortable hitting right-handed. It took him many years of awkward swinging from the left side before he could hit the ball hard.

When Pete started high school, he thought he would have no trouble in sports. Although he was a tough athlete, he was too small to play on the football team his first year. Disappointed, he spent his sophomore year fooling around and flunked his classes. He dropped out of school, but returned the following year, ready to pay attention. But sports were still his main interest, and Pete battled his way onto the high school football and baseball teams and became a starter.

Because he had spent an extra year in high school, Pete was not able to play on the school's baseball team during his final year. So he joined an amateur league, where he began stinging line drives to the outfield. The league was not an important one, and

Pete could not attract much attention from the pro scouts. But his uncle, Buddy Bloebaum, happened to be a scout for the Cincinnati Reds, a team that played near Pete's hometown. Buddy arranged a tryout for Pete.

A day of hitting and fielding in the uniform of his favorite team seemed like a dream come true for Pete. But this was only the start. That summer of 1960, the Reds offered him a contract. Because it was well into the season, the Reds thought Pete might want to wait until next spring and start fresh. Little did they know about Pete Rose! He jumped at their offer and reported immediately to the Reds' Class D team in Geneva, New York.

There Pete discovered how rough the road to the major leagues can be. Though Geneva was the lowest step on the Reds' minor league ladder, Pete was inexperienced and really had to struggle. His hitting was only fair and his fielding was sloppy. Pete chalked up 36 errors in just 86 games! The Reds' minor league coaches had to strain to think of good things to report about the frail-looking Rose kid.

To make matters worse, teammates resented this newcomer at first. They did not like it when Tony

Perez, the popular second baseman, was moved to a new position to make room for Pete. Some thought Pete's all-out hustle was just a way of showing off. But it did not take long before Pete's hustle and enthusiasm began to win over his coaches and teammates.

Soon after he began in the minors, Pete began to hit the ball well from both sides of the plate. Rose moved up quickly through the Reds' system, doing well at Tampa, Florida, and Macon, Georgia.

Although he worked hard in the minors, Pete always found time to joke around and make friends with the players. Once he and a teammate had trouble grabbing the catcher's high throws to second base. The next day the catcher found Pete and his friend standing on a stepladder, waiting for his throws to second!

As Pete worked his way up through the minors, both his body and his skills developed. He no longer was the skinny kid who fumbled ground balls. The most important man that Pete impressed was Fred Hutchinson, the Cincinnati manager. No matter what skills Pete lacked, Hutchinson loved his all-out effort. A manager's main job is to keep players trying their hardest all the time. With Pete, a manager's job was easy.

At spring training camp in 1963, Pete was expected to win a promotion to the Reds' top minor league team. Since it was before the regular season, major and minor leaguers practiced together. One day Pete, who was not on the list of those who would take part in an afternoon exhibition game, was told by a friend to suit up anyway, just in case the Reds needed an extra player.

Pete did just that. Whenever Manager Hutchinson turned around, there was Rose staring up at him. Pete was so anxious to play he must have looked like a puppy begging to go outside. The game went into extra innings, and, sure enough, Pete was finally called on to pinch-hit. When Pete smacked a double, Hutchinson decided to keep him in the game. In the 14th inning, Pete lined another double and scored the winning run. By the end of training camp, Pete had Hutchinson convinced. After less than three years in the minors, Pete became a Cincinnati Red.

During 1963, his first year in the pros, there was no end to surprises. Pete found himself starting at second base and leading off for the Reds' first game of the year! The nervous rookie drew a walk from the pitcher. But Pete never "walks" anywhere on the

Pete, 1963 National League Rookie of the Year, and Chicago
White Sox pitcher Gary Peters, 1963 American League Rookie,
pose with their trophies.

field. For the first time, Cincinnati fans were treated
to Pete's unusual all-out dash to first on a walk.
Again there were people who thought he was a hot
dog and a showboat. But Pete kept running all year
long. He finished with a .273 average and won Rookie
of the Year honors in the National League.

The year 1963 had been a good one, but Pete
found he still had much to learn in 1964. He was

bothered by frustrating batting slumps. As a second baseman, he had trouble getting the ball back to first base on double-play balls. Cincinnati lost the pennant by just one game that year, and Pete felt that his troubles may have cost the Reds a chance at the pennant.

Determined to improve, Pete traveled to Caracas, Venezuela, to play winter baseball. He did not exactly become an instant hero there. In one inning he blew four fielding attempts before the side was retired! South American fans booed him loudly at first, but Pete continued to work hard and gained extra experience at his sport.

In 1965 Pete's hitting improved. He batted .312 and was voted to the All-Star team. But Pete realized that he was not cut out to be a second baseman. He had grown to 190 pounds, and his hard-charging, bullish style seemed more suited to another position. After playing third base in 1966, Pete moved to the outfield. From there Pete moved steadily to the top as a champion singles hitter.

During Pete's first years with the Reds, the major leagues were full of muscular hitters. They swung hard and could blast tremendous home runs out of the park. These hitters gained the most attention and earned the highest salaries. Soon other batters began to try for home runs instead of singles and doubles. As a result, many thought the game had become a slugging match with too few batters getting on base.

In baseball today, a .300 average is the least that one can expect from a good hitter. But in the 1960s very few people even reached that level. Carl Yastrzemski actually won the American League batting title in 1968 hitting only .301.

Pete was one player who brought "scientific hitting" back to baseball. He felt that a person who got two or three hits in a game was just as important as the player who hit home runs some of the time and struck out most of the time. A person who hits for a higher average gets on base more and has a better chance to score more runs. Rather than swing for home runs, Pete tried to make sure he always hit the ball. He swung hard but did not try to kill the ball.

With his success and colorful style, Pete became one of the few singles hitters to draw attention. In both 1968 and 1969, Pete led the National League in hitting by slim margins going into the final games.

Pete races for second against the Atlanta Braves.

Both times he came through with important hits that earned him the title. In 1968 he beat out Matty Alou of the Pittsburgh Pirates with a .335 average. The next year his .347 mark edged out the Pirates' Roberto Clemente.

Pete had once predicted that he would become the first singles hitter to earn $100,000 a year. By 1970 his prediction came true, and no one could have been more proud. Pete had proved that scientific hitting paid off.

Pete felt more comfortable in the outfield than on second base and made only three fielding errors in 1968. He also threw out 20 runners while they were trying to make extra bases on hits to the outfield.

In 1970 Pete won the Golden Glove award as the outstanding fielder at his position. He had come quite a long way from his fumble-fingered days in the minor leagues at Geneva!

In the 1970s, the Cincinnati lineup was known as the Big Red Machine because the players cranked out so many runs. Pete took special pride in being the lead-off batter of this lineup. When he reached base, such sluggers as Johnny Bench, Tony Perez, and Lee May could drive him in.

As a contact hitter, Pete seldom strikes out.

Shortstop Bert Campaneris of the Oakland A's tags Rose at
second base during game six of the 1972 World Series.

Though the Reds' pitching was rarely above average, they slugged their way to the top of the
Western Division of the National League. In 1970
they advanced to the World Series but were thrashed
by the Baltimore Orioles. In 1972 the Reds again
made it to the World Series, this time against the
Oakland A's. The two teams battled to a tie before
Oakland won the seventh and final game.

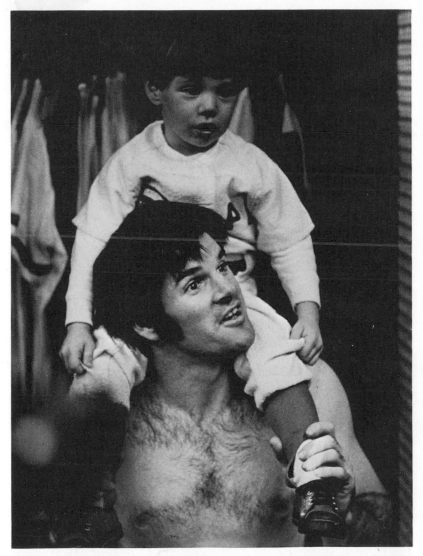

Two-year-old Petey Rose sits on his father's shoulders in the
Red's locker room after the game.

In 1973 the Big Red Machine came out on top of their division again, but they fizzled in the playoffs. Pete did his share by winning his third batting title with a .338 average. He was also voted the National League's Most Valuable Player for his efforts. By now, Charlie Hustle was famous throughout the sports world.

Whether he was on the field, on a bus, in bed, or in the locker room, Pete could not seem to sit still. One of his teammates, Tommy Helms, recalls an event that became commonplace. When Cincinnati was on the road, Tommy would wake up in the hotel room to see Pete, pajamas and all, practicing his batting stance in bed. Pete wanted to get in his batting practice no matter where he happened to be!

As a base runner, Pete loved to take a chance. Any time a ball was hit to the outfield, he looked to see if he could try for an extra base. It was usually a close play when he tried, and Pete always sailed headfirst into the dirt to reach the bag. That method is not the easiest on the body. But winning came first to Pete, his body came second. If a head-first dive was the fastest way to the bag, that was the only way to slide. Pete's peppery spirit and effort

The Red's Charlie Hustle knocks third base loose after sliding head first under the tag of Phillie third baseman Mike Schmidt.

rubbed off on his teammates. It was hard for them to loaf when Pete Rose was always out there hustling.

Even in games that were not close, Pete refused to quit trying. Pete will never forget seeing a game when a team led 7 to 0 in the ninth inning. An infielder for the team dawdled just a little on an easy ground ball hit, thinking the game was as good as won. The runner managed to beat the throw to first. The losing team began to rally. By the time the inning was over, the fielder's team had lost by a score of 8 to 7. Pete says that this game is a good reminder to him to make a habit of hustling so that he will never let up at an important time.

Some people think Pete goes too far at times. One of the most famous examples of his hustle came in the 1972 All-Star game. In the bottom of the 12th inning, Pete came to bat with the score tied. He singled and moved to second on another hit. When the next batter also singled to center field, Pete barreled around third base and headed for home. He knew he was taking a chance, but if he scored the game would be over. Center fielder Amos Otis of Kansas City threw the ball to Cleveland catcher Ray Fosse. Fosse, who stood 6 feet, 3 inches, weighed 220 pounds, and was blocking home plate. Just as the ball arrived, Pete blasted full speed into the catcher. Caps, gloves, bodies, and the baseball went flying. Pete was called safe and his team won the game, but, unfortunately, Fosse was seriously injured.

Opponents and fans in other ball parks had to admire Pete's spirit. But, popular as he was, Pete also found himself the target of hatred. As usual,

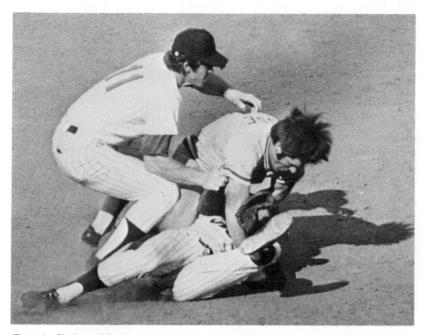

Pete's fight with New York Met shortstop Bud Harrelson in the third game of the 1973 National League Play-offs cleared both benches as players rushed to help their teammates.

his Charlie Hustle style was the cause. Pete was on first base late in a play-off game against the New York Mets in 1973. It was an important game, and the Reds were losing 9 to 2. The next Cincinnati batter hit a hard grounder. This gave the Mets a perfect chance to throw Rose out at second and the batter out at first. Pete knew that he had reached second base too late. But he wanted to keep shortstop Bud

Harrelson from making the throw back to first for the second out. Rose crashed into Harrelson, who thought Rose had slid a little *too* hard. In a second, the two were fighting. The little shortstop was no match for Pete, who quickly got the upper hand.

Angry New York fans threw garbage and bottles at Rose when the Reds took their positions in the field. The situation became so dangerous that the Reds had to leave the field until things returned to normal. During a few games after that fans threw things at "Bully" Rose. But Rose and Harrelson patched things up, and soon the fans forgot the fight.

Though the Reds' hitting had been good in the early 1970s, it had become even better by 1975. Rose, Perez, and Bench still scored more than their share of runs. They were joined by superstars George Foster and Joe Morgan. In order to help the team, Pete again moved to a new position. He dusted off his third baseman's mitt to make way for the talented outfielder Ken Griffey.

That year Cincinnati trampled the other teams in their division. They won 108 games and lost only 54. This put them a comfortable 20 games in front of the second-place team. In the 1975 World Series,

During 1975 World Series action, Pete slides safely into third. In this Series, Pete tore up Red Sox pitching with ten hits for a .370 average.

Cincinnati battled the Boston Red Sox in one of the most exciting series ever. There were late-inning rallies, extra-inning home runs, and close plays that decided several games. In the final game, Cincinnati came from behind to nose out Boston 4 games to 3. Pete and his mates had finally won the championship! Pete had helped the cause by batting .357 in the play-offs and a sizzling .370 in the World Series.

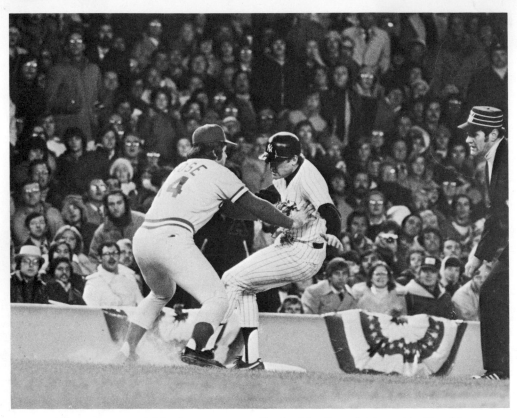

Pete tags out Yankee runner Graig Nettles during the Reds'
fourth and final victory over New York in the 1976 Series.

The following year, 1976, the Reds proved themselves to be one of the top teams in baseball history.
After winning their division again, they crushed a
fine Phillies team in three straight games to win the
play-off. Then they went on to beat the New York
Yankees four games in a row to win another World
Series!

By 1977 Pete was a 36-year-old veteran who had played 14 seasons with the Reds. At that age, most athletes begin to lose their skills. They start to rest themselves more during the year, and sometimes their batting average begins to drop. A good number of players retire when they reach their mid-30s. But for Pete, the best was yet to come. In 1977 the old-timer refused to slow down. In fact, he played in 162 games, more than anyone in the league. And toward the end of the season, when some athletes start to wear out, Pete was at his strongest. Because he stayed in such good shape, he was still ready to hustle in the big games during September and October.

Pete is very concerned about staying in shape. He does not smoke or drink. He also gets plenty of rest, often sleeping until noon. Before games he stays off his feet so his legs will be fresh.

Though Pete is a big star with lots of money, he lets nothing get in the way of baseball. Some call him a sports nut. He follows every bit of news about baseball and knows weeks in advance which pitchers he is likely to face. After playing a tough game for the Reds, he often listened to the final innings of other games on the radio. Sometimes he

Teammate Joe Morgan signals for Pete to "stand up" rather than slide to score a Cincinnati run.

Pete laces hit #3,000 on May 5, 1978, during a game against the Montreal Expos and Steve Rogers.

even videotaped ball games while he was on road trips so he could watch them when he returned.

In 1978 Pete won more attention than ever. He belted his 3,000th hit early in the year. Pete was only the 13th person to ever reach that goal. Later that year, Pete went on a batting streak. "When you're in a slump, any pitcher can get you out," Pete once said. "When you're hot, you can hit anyone." Slumps and streaks are a strange part of baseball. No one knows why or how they happen. Pete has been through both many times. He has put together strings of 20, 22, and 24 games in a row with at least one hit.Yet in the spring of 1978, Pete was bogged down in one of his worst slumps. He had managed just five hits in his last 44 trips to the plate. That comes out to a .113 average, which is pitiful for a major league player.

Then on June 14, 1978, Pete came out of his slump and banged out two hits in four at-bats against the Chicago Cubs. The next night he had two more hits. And the next night. Game after game, Pete managed at least one safe hit. Some of the National League's finest pitchers tried to end the streak. Hard-throwing Vida Blue of San Francisco, J. R. Richard of Houston, sinker-ball pitcher Tommy John of Los Angeles, and Montreal's tough Steve Rogers all had their chances. But no one could hold Pete without a hit. Finally, Pete's streak reached 36 games—one game short of

Pete connects and turns to sprint toward first base.

the National League record set by Tommy Holmes. This record had not been matched in 33 years!

In the next game at the Mets' Shea Stadium, Pete wasted no time in getting his share of the record. He socked two line singles early in the game to tie Holmes' mark. The following night, the national spotlight was on Pete as he went for the record. Again he broke the suspense early and came up with not one but three hits! Fans everywhere cheered, and the streak lasted 40, 42, then 44 games.

Under such pressure, many athletes become tense and unpleasant. But to watch Pete perform, you would have thought it was all one big party. "The play-offs are pressure, this is fun," he told reporters. Pete proved that the pressure did not seem to affect him. In 6 of the games he didn't get his hit until his last trip to the plate! Through it all, Pete remained cheerful and pleasant and was especially careful to include the former record-holder, Holmes, in the attention.

Joe DiMaggio had set an all-time major league record by hitting safely in 56 straight games. It was the only streak in the record books longer than Pete's. Entering the 45th game of his streak on, Pete had his sights on the 56-game hitting record that some thought would never be challenged. The Reds played against the Braves in Atlanta. The pitcher, Larry McWilliams, pitched carefully to Pete from the beginning. Pete drew a walk in the first inning. His second time up he met a pitch solidly and drilled a line drive up the middle. McWilliams stabbed at the ball by sheer reflex and came up with it. Rose was out. On his third trip to the plate, Pete grounded out. On his fourth at-bat, he faced relief pitcher Gene Garber. Pete knew he was running out of chances. He swung hard at a pitch and smashed another line drive. Unfortunately, the Braves' third baseman, Bob Horner, happened to be in the right spot and grabbed the ball for the out.

But luck did not seem to be with Pete. He had hit two balls as well as they could be hit and still his streak was in danger. In the ninth inning, Pete made one last trip to the batter's box. With two outs, he knew that this was his last chance. The count on Pete was two balls and two strikes when Garber wound up and threw. Pete swung and missed, and his incredible streak was finally stopped. During that streak, Pete had really earned his hits. In 198 times at bat, he had hit only one pop fly and had struck out only three times.

At the end of the 1978 season, Pete said goodbye to the team that had been his favorite since his boyhood days. He still loved the Reds and Cincinnati, but changes were taking place on the team. Pete did not agree with some things that were being done by the Reds' management. He also did not think they were paying him what he was worth. So Rose became a *free agent*. This meant that other teams could offer him contracts, and he could sign the one that looked best to him.

Pete was taking a chance by becoming a free agent because 38-year-old players are usually considered too old to be of much value. But Pete did not show the usual signs of growing old. Several teams joined in a bidding match to try and win Pete for their team. Some offered him up to a million dollars a year! Others found out that Pete was a horse-racing fan and offered to give him race horses along with a huge salary. In the end, money was not the most important thing for Pete. In fact, he took the lowest of the final offers and signed with the Philadelphia Phillies.

Above all, Pete loves to win. He knew the Phillies had plenty of talent and would be contenders. He also had friends in Philadelphia and knew some of the team's players. Even though he was an excellent third baseman, Pete worked hard in Philadelphia learning to play yet another position—first base. If that was what his new manager wanted him to do, he would give it his best.

The player who wanted to become baseball's first

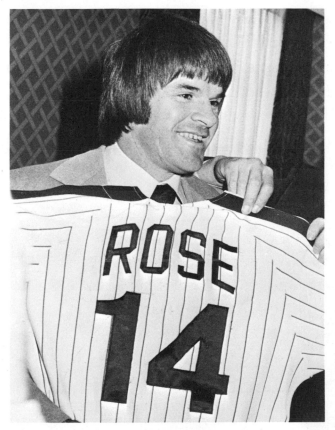

Pete with his new Philadelphia Phillie uniform

$100,000-a-year singles hitter was now far past that goal. He had become an $800,000-a-year singles hitter. The Phillies felt he was worth it. Very simply, they knew that Pete was one of the most exciting players in baseball.

For the Phillies, it was not just his many records and championships that made Pete worth $800,000 a year. Sure, he had led the National League in hits six times and in games played, at-bats, runs, and doubles four times each. True, he had won three batting titles and had been voted Most Valuable Player once. And the record books did have him

Charlie Hustle steals second and looks to the umpire for the call.

Pete congratulates teammate Bake McBride after a McBride home run.

listed as the man with the most singles in history. He had also been selected to the All Star team at *four* different positions: second base, third base, outfield, and first base. But Pete would be most valuable to the Phillies as the man they called Charlie Hustle—a player who could put a spark in the other players on the team.

If the Phillies had expected magic from Rose, their hopes were soon dashed. Although Pete was awarded some important individual honors, in 1979 the talented Phillies lost nearly as many games as they won—84 wins to 78 losses. For the tenth time in his career, Pete banged out over 200 hits in a season. This broke the previous record of nine 200-hit years held by the great Ty Cobb. Pete was also honored as baseball's "Player of the Decade" for the 1970s by a *Baseball Magazine* poll.

But for a team player such as Rose, the main goal was to win another World Series. For most of the following season, it seemed as if Pete's indifferent teammates could not catch Rose's enthusiasm. But on the next to the last day of the season, a late-season push lifted Philadelphia to the divisional title over Montreal.

The National League play-off against Houston was a wild affair with leads changing hands nearly every inning. Pete helped to win one game with a play that reminded many of the 1970 All-Star game. In the fourth game, Rose raced around third base on a ball hit to the outfield and headed for home. He slammed into the Astros' catcher Bruce Bochy and

Pete rips into one to score another hit.

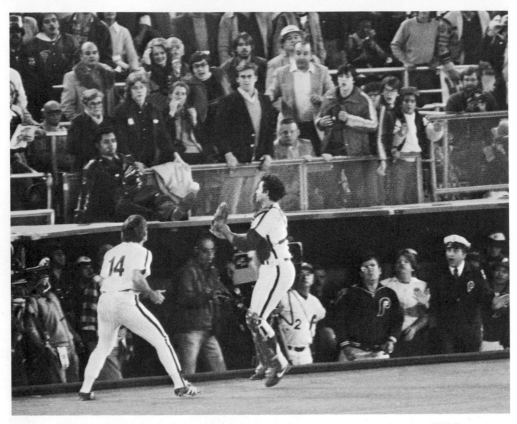

During the ninth inning of Philadelphia's fourth win in the 1980 Series, Pete gets ready to grab a foul pop-up deflected by Phillie catcher Bob Boone.

scored the winning run on a close play. But Philadelphia finally took the series three games to two.

In the 1980 World Series, Pete at first had little luck against Kansas City. But in the sixth and final game of the Series, he stroked three hits in four at-bats. Even more memorable was a typical example of Pete's hustle. His team was leading 4 to 2 in the ninth, but the Royals loaded the bases. With only one out, Kansas City's Frank White hit a foul pop up near first base. Phillies' catcher Bob Boone trotted under the ball, but the ball hit his mitt and bounced out. Fortunately Rose was just a foot away. He reached over and grabbed the ball before it hit the ground. One out later, the Phillies were leaping for joy. They had won the Phillies' first World Series in the team's 97-year history.

Above all, Pete is a leader. He works hard and sets a good example for younger teammates. Pete loves the game of baseball and works for the club at different events during the off-season. He enjoys fans because he can remember when he was one. He willingly gives out autographs and often throws balls into the midst of cheering fans.

Pete has made a name for himself in baseball out of hustle and hard work. But best of all, he plays the game with enthusiasm. Some of baseball's old-timers say that modern-day players are spoiled by making so much money. But they do not say that about Pete Rose. He always gives the fans their money's worth because he always plays to win.

Doffing his cap, Pete acknowledges the standing ovation of Phillie fans after his 200th hit in 1979. The hit broke Ty Cobb's record and gave Pete ten 200-hit seasons.

44

BASEBALL 3,000 HITTERS

In 1979 when Lou Brock and Carl Yastrzemski made their 3,000th hits, they joined Pete Rose in a select group of only 15 players. By the end of his career, Rose may advance in the standings to either tie or replace the great home-run hitter, Hank Aaron, and rank second to the legendary Ty Cobb.

1. TY COBB
   Detroit Tigers (1905-1928)
   4,191 hits - #3,000 in 1922

2. HANK AARON
   Milwaukee & Atlanta Braves (1954-1976)
   3,771 hits - #3,000 in 1968

3. STAN MUSIAL
   St. Louis Cardinals (1941-1963)
   3,630 hits - #3,000 in 1958

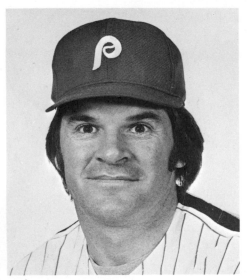

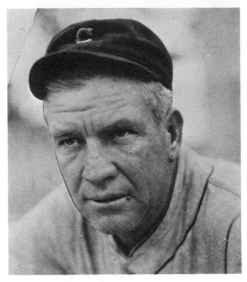

4. PETE ROSE
   Cincinnati Reds &
   Philadelphia Phillies (1963-   )
   3,557 hits - #3,000 in 1978

5. TRIS SPEAKER
   Cleveland Indians (1907-1928)
   3,515 hits - #3,000 in 1925

6. HONUS WAGNER
   Pittsburgh Pirates (1897-1917)
   3,430 hits - #3,000 in 1914

7. EDDIE COLLINS
   Philadelphia Athletics &
   Chicago White Sox (1906-1930)
   3,311 hits - #3,000 in 1925

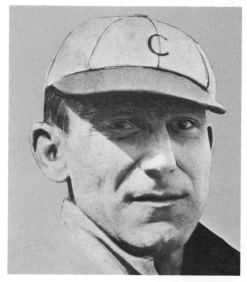

8. WILLIE MAYS
   New York & San Francisco Giants
   (1951-1973)
   3,283 hits - #3,000 in 1970

9. NAP LAJOIE
   Cleveland Indians (1896-1916)
   3,251 hits - #3,000 in 1914

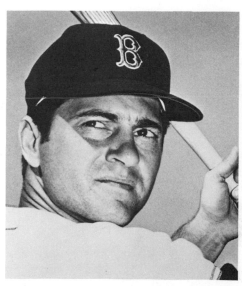

10. PAUL WANER
    Pittsburgh Pirates (1926-1945)
    3,152 hits - #3,000 in 1942

11. CARL YASTRZEMSKI
    Boston Red Sox (1961-   )
    3,109 hits - #3,000 in 1979

12. CAP ANSON
    Chicago Colts (1876-1897)
    3,041 hits - #3,000 in 1897

13. LOU BROCK
    St. Louis Cardinals (1961-1979)
    3,023 hits - #3,000 in 1979

14. AL KALINE
    Detroit Tigers (1953-1974)
    3,007 hits - #3,000 in 1974

15. ROBERTO CLEMENTE
    Pittsburgh Pirates (1955-1972)
    3,000 hits - #3,000 in 1972